Tops and tales

by Primrose Lockwood and Christine Laskey,
John Gordon, Stan Cullimore, Moira Andrew, Jan Needle

Illustrated by Josephine Marston

Compiled and edited by Wendy Body

LONGMAN

TOBY
and other
tales

Contents

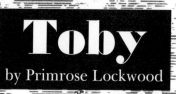

Toby

by Primrose Lockwood

Toby

by Primrose Lockwood

The dog had nowhere to go and no home.
It was winter and cold to be out of doors with no
comfortable bed to sleep in and no proper food.
Some nights he slept in a barn or a stable yard, but
next morning he moved on again. In appearance
he was like a sheepdog and his colouring was black
and brown and white.

Late in December he came to the outskirts of
a town. One night he slept in a bus shelter and the
next in a shop doorway. In the day he fed off scraps
from dustbins, but there wasn't enough and he was
still hungry.

One day he wandered into a school playground.
A girl called Jessie, sitting by an upstairs window,
looked out and saw the dog. She was new to the
school and, as she hadn't yet made any friends, she
felt lonely. Seeing the dog made her think of her
grandparents' dog back in the village where she
used to live. She felt happy for a while.

When playtime came she stood in the
playground stamping her feet and banging her
hands to keep warm. She didn't run around like
most of the children did because she still felt too shy
to join in their games. Towards the end of playtime

she walked over to the old bicycle shed and saw the dog lying on the cold ground, sleeping. When she bent over him, she saw that his coat was matted and broken sticks were caught in his tail. For a moment, he lifted up his head and looked at her. She watched him lying there and wondered how she could help him.

Jessie was late getting back into class. Only Daniel and Emma, who were always last, were still taking off their coats. In the classroom the children were sitting round the room, reading.

"Come and read, Jessie," said the teacher, seeing her. Jessie read two pages of her reading book. She liked reading if her book was interesting but this one wasn't.

"You've read very nicely," said her teacher. "How are you getting on Jessie? Are you happy here?"

"Yes," said Jessie. She couldn't have said that yesterday, not truthfully. But today, after seeing the dog, she did feel happy – happy to have something to care about, happy that she might be able to help him.

At dinnertime, Jessie sat at a table in the dining-room eating her sandwiches. Today they were cheese ones. Mostly they were cheese, though sometimes they were peanut butter. She liked cheese but today she only ate three of them, leaving the fourth in her sandwich box.

'I'll save my apple for later,' thought Jessie and stood up.

"Please can I go out now?" she said to the dinner lady.

Jessie thought that she was going to say no and that she must wait until everyone else had finished, but she didn't. She was friendly and said, "Go on then."

Alone in the playground Jessie ran over to the bicycle shed, still carrying her sandwich box.

"Don't let the dog have gone," she thought.

The dog was still there, lying down but not sleeping. He turned his head for a moment and looked at Jessie, then rested it down again on his front paws.

"Good boy," she whispered, in the kind of voice that her grandparents used when they spoke to their dog, Muffin. She put out her hand and stroked him for a while. When she stopped, the dog nudged her gently with his nose.

"All right," she said. "I'll stroke you for a bit longer."

She gave the dog the sandwich she had saved. He ate it quickly and Jessie felt sorry that she had no more to give him.

"If you're still here tomorrow, I'll bring you something else to eat," she said.

At hometime Jessie took as long as she could putting on her coat.

"Haven't you gone yet?" said the teacher.

"I'm nearly ready, Miss Bramwell," said Jessie.

Her feet clattered on the stone stairs as she ran down them. There were two parents standing in the playground, talking. Their children were chasing about near them, but they were a long way from the bicycle shed and they didn't notice Jessie run over to it and go in. The dog was still there, but he was sleeping. One of his paws twitched slightly when Jessie patted him.

"I'll see you again tomorrow," she said.

Jessie thought about the dog all evening. She helped her mother and father decorate the Christmas tree and looked at the lights and coloured ornaments shining in the darkness, but she didn't forget him. She thought she might tell her parents about the dog. She thought she might say, 'Mum, Dad, I saw a dog at school today. He hasn't got a home. Can we have him?'

But in the end she didn't. They might have said she couldn't have him. Then she wouldn't have been able to hope any more. Now at least she could dream. She saw the dog lying on the rug next to the fire while she brushed the tangles from his coat.

"Last day at school tomorrow, Jessie," said Dad at bedtime. "Are you pleased?"

"Yes," said Jessie.

"But you like it there, don't you, Jessie?" said Mum.

"Yes," she said and then she thought, "Yes, I like it now I've seen the dog."

Next morning Jessie walked along the road to school. She didn't live far away, only a few houses along. Since she'd started there, usually she set off at the last minute so as not to have too long in the playground. But this morning was different.

"I think I'll go to school early today," she had said.

Her mother had given her two parcels to put in her bag, one containing sandwiches to eat at dinnertime and the other things to eat at the party in the afternoon, a chocolate cake and some biscuits.

"Do dogs like chocolate cake?" Jessie wondered. "They like biscuits. Muffin does anyway. He takes them out of my hand."

There weren't many children in the playground and no one bothered to look at Jessie on her way to the bicycle shed.

"Please still be there," she whispered. "I want you to be there more than anything."

The dog was standing alert, watching, waiting. When he saw Jessie, he put his head down and wriggled his body in an excited sort of way, wagging his tail.

"I told you I'd come," she said. He felt cold when she stroked him. Then she crouched down and unwrapped one of the parcels, letting him eat two of the cheese sandwiches intended for dinnertime. He began to sniff at the other parcel, pushing his nose into it.

"That's the chocolate cake," she said. "Oh all right, you can have some of it if you want." She took it out of the wrapping and broke a piece off for him.

Jessie suddenly felt guilty. She couldn't give the cake in for the party any more, not with some of it broken off. She would just have to give in the biscuits instead. They wouldn't miss the cake. She felt sure the other children would bring lots of things to eat. She began to feel a bit better about it. The dog needed it more than the children did.

The school bell rang. Jessie knew she must go into school but first she decided to take her coat off and put it down on the floor in the corner of the bicycle shed for the dog to lie on.

"This will keep you warm," she said. "This is better than lying on the cold stone." She watched him settle down on it, then went into school.

"Party things on the table by the window," called Miss Bramwell when Jessie went into the classroom.

Jessie put the biscuits down on the table quickly, hoping that no one was noticing what she had brought. She could see some tins that probably contained cakes or buns and a box that had a chocolate cake picture on the top.

"It won't be as nice as my home-made one,"

thought Jessie. "It's only a shop cake." The dog had liked her cake. She was glad there was still some left in her bag which she could give him later.

At playtime, when the teacher saw Jessie going down the stairs without her coat on, she said, "Go back and put your coat on, Jessie. It's freezing outside."

Jessie looked at Miss Bramwell, not knowing what to say.

"I think she's lost it," said Lucy, a girl from Jessie's class, going down behind her. "Her peg's next to mine. It wasn't there."

"Take her down to Lost Property then, Lucy, please," said Miss Bramwell. "If hers isn't there, let her borrow another one to keep her warm."

At the lost property box at the back of the hall Jessie looked for the coat that she knew wasn't there. She went out into the playground wearing a strange one.

Later in the day Jessie sat next to Lucy at the party. It was quite a nice party really, much better than she had expected. She didn't feel as shy and left out as usual. The teacher was playing a tape of Christmas carols, 'Away in a manger, no crib for a bed ...'

"I wish Toby had a manger to lie in," thought Jessie. For the first time she realised that she'd thought of him not just as 'the dog', but by a name.

Toby seemed to suit him. There was a dog called Toby in one of her books at home. Jessie thought it was a lovely name for a dog. Now she had a dog of her own to call Toby ... Jessie pushed it out of her mind that he might not be her dog for much longer.

"Look, Jessie," called Lucy, interrupting her thoughts. "Look out of the window. It's snowing."

Some of the children rushed over to the window to look out. Jessie stayed in her place and watched the flakes of snow floating gently down. Jessie loved snow. For a moment she felt the excitement she had always felt when she saw the first snow of winter. Then she remembered Toby, with the snow blowing into the open door of the bicycle shed.

At hometime the teacher said, "Could your coat be in the dining-room, Jessie?"

"No," said Jessie.

Miss Bramwell walked along the empty corridor looking for one left behind.

"You'd better go home in the coat from Lost Property," she said at last. "No one seems to want it. But bring it back after Christmas."

Jessie went down the stairs feeling guilty. She hadn't actually told a lie. She hadn't actually said,

"I've lost my coat, Miss Bramwell."

Miss Bramwell had just thought she must have. But she hadn't been completely honest. She had let Miss Bramwell think she'd lost it.

'Oh I hope it's keeping Toby warm,' thought Jessie.

It was still snowing. She liked to feel the snow on her. She liked to look up and see it coming down. The playground already had a thin covering on it. She looked at the footprints her shoes made. She was glad she couldn't see any paw prints in the snow.

The dog heard Jessie coming and sat up, alert once more, waiting.

"I've come," she said and for the first time put her arms round him and hugged him.

She fed him the rest of the chocolate cake until it was all gone. He licked the crumbs off the paper and would have eaten the paper too if Jessie hadn't taken it away from him.

"No, no, Toby," she said. "That's your name now – Toby." She wondered if he liked it. He wagged his tail so she thought he must do. Then she picked up her own coat and put the one from Lost Property on the floor instead.

"It's better to go home with a coat that's dirty!" she thought, than to go home with someone else's. When she put it on it felt warm.

"I'll come back tomorrow, Toby," she said. "I'll bring you some food then." She patted him and went out into the yard. The dog started to follow her.

"No, go back, Toby," she said, looking at the snow

beginning to fall on his head. "Go back," she said, pushing him inside.

Jessie walked through the empty playground, trying not to think of someone else's coat lying on the ground, trying not to think about the snow getting deeper.

Inside her house, Jessie sat by the front window and watched people coming home from work in the snow. It looked beautiful out. Though before she'd seen the dog she had wanted it to snow for Christmas, now she felt sad when she thought of him with no proper shelter.

Should she tell mum and dad after all, for Toby's sake? No, no, she couldn't. She wouldn't let herself think of it.

"Mum, Dad, can I walk along the road as far as school?" asked Jessie. "It doesn't look properly dark yet. I want to see what the snow looks like in the school playground."

"All right," they said, "if you're not long." Dad found Jessie's wellingtons. She put them on with some extra socks inside. Then she put some biscuits in her coat pocket and went out.

She didn't know how she was going to get to Toby. She just knew she wanted to see him, to make sure he was all right now it was snowing again. She wouldn't go into the yard, just call to him if no one was around. She could stroke him through the railings.

There was hardly anyone in the street, just some children further along. They wouldn't hear when she called Toby and the people in the houses across the street had got their curtains closed.

"Toby," she called, not too loudly, but loud enough for him to hear her. For a moment she didn't think he was going to come. Then he appeared round the side of the school building. She couldn't see him clearly until he was right up to her.

"Toby," she said. "Are you all right in the snow?"

He put his nose through the railings and ate the biscuits she held out to him. Then she patted him. A thin covering of snow was on his back and head and tail. She wiped the snow off his head with her mittened hand.

Jessie woke up early. The clock on the dressing table had luminous fingers and pointed to half past six. She got out of bed and put her clothes on quickly. Downstairs, she put on her coat and the woolly hat, scarf and mittens given to her by Grandma and Grandad. She turned the key of the back door and went into the porch to put on her wellingtons. They felt icy cold. Jessie shivered. She tried to pull back the bolt on the porch door but it was right at the top and too high for her to reach it properly. She fetched a stool from the kitchen to stand on. The bolt was stiff but she managed to pull it back.

Snow had blown against the outside of the porch door and some fell inside when she pulled it open. It looked deeper than the night before. The street lamps were on as it was still dark. Jessie looked up and saw flakes of snow falling in the brightness of the lamplight.

'I'll go inside the playground,' thought Jessie. It didn't occur to her that the gates might not be open. She only wanted to see Toby, make sure the snow hadn't come too far into the doorway where he was and give him the piece of cheese she had taken from the fridge.

But the gates were locked. She looked through them at the school building. It was so different in the snow, everywhere deserted.

'The caretaker can't be up yet,' thought Jessie. 'It's too early for the gates to be open.'

Then she remembered it was the holidays. 'They probably won't be opened at all,' thought Jessie.

While she was standing there thinking this, a boy called Matthew was coming along the road, having finished his paper round. He was older than Jessie. He was surprised to see the small, lonely figure standing by the gates – not moving, just staring in. The boy recognised her as the new girl in his sister Lucy's class.

"What are you doing out so early?" he said.

Jessie turned round, startled to see Matthew. She was afraid that he might find out about Toby. She didn't answer.

"Don't be afraid," Matthew said. "You're Jessie, aren't you, Lucy's new friend? I'm her brother Matthew."

She knew he was. She had seen him in the garden with Lucy, just two houses along from hers. It sounded wonderful to Jessie being called anyone's friend, but especially Lucy's. For a moment the scared look left her face.

"Won't you tell me what you're doing?" he said again.

"I'm ..." Jessie hesitated. She didn't know what to say. She didn't want to tell him a lie, but how could she tell the truth?

Matthew waited, watching the snow falling on the upturned face of the child next to him.

Finally she spoke.

"I've come to feed my dog," she said.

"Your dog?" said Matthew.

"My dog," said Jessie. "He used to be a stray, but he's mine now. He's in the bicycle shed." She called out to Toby then and soon he came running across to her in the snow, full of eagerness to see her and hungry for what she had brought him.

"Are you sure he's a stray?" asked Matthew.

"I'm sure he was," said Jessie. "But he's mine now like I told you. I've been feeding him. I need to get him out of the bicycle shed now it's the holidays, but I can't because the gates are locked."

"If you managed to get him out, would you take him home?" asked Matthew.

"No," said Jessie.

"Why not?" he asked.

"They might not let me keep him."

"But you can't keep him like this forever."

"I know," said Jessie. She had known it all along really, but she had never allowed herself to think it before.

"Please," said Jessie, "help me to find somewhere safe for him. Help me to find somewhere safe for him until Christmas is over. Let him be my dog for Christmas."

"He can go in our hut," said Matthew.

"Can he?" said Jessie, hopefully.

"Yes," said Matthew. "But only until after Christmas. You'll have to tell then. Will you promise you'll tell then?"

"I promise," said Jessie.

Matthew walked along with Jessie as far as her house. "We'll get Toby out over the field wall at the back of the school," he said. "He'll have been out that way while you've not been there. We can get on to the field through our garden."

"Can we go for him now?" asked Jessie.

"No, not now," said Matthew. "Call for us about half past nine or ten, and we'll go then."

Jessie walked along the path and banged her wellingtons, one at a time, against the wall by the porch door to knock the snow off them. 'You'll soon be warm now, Toby,' she thought. 'It will be better in a hut than a bicycle shed.'

In the house, Jessie's mum was coming downstairs.

"Are you up already?" she said. "Have you been out in the garden to play in the snow?"

"Yes," said Jessie. "I've been out in the snow."

'If only I could tell,' thought Jessie. 'If only I could tell.'

Soon there was no trace of Jessie's footprints for the snow had covered them.

At half past nine Jessie knocked on Lucy's and Matthew's door. It was still snowing. It wasn't bright now it was day but the greyness didn't bother Jessie. She felt excited about making a better home for Toby. In her excitement she almost forgot it was Christmas Eve.

Lucy answered the door. She was dressed in red and looked Christmassy.

Jessie felt shy. She wondered if Matthew had told her about Toby.

Then Lucy said, "I can't wait to see Toby." She had a book in her hand. Halfway up the stairs a black cat was washing itself.

Lucy led the way across the hallway, into the kitchen. Jessie looked round. She was interested in houses. Then she remembered she ought to have taken her wellingtons off, but it was too late now. She had already left bits of snow on the hall carpet.

Matthew was sitting in the kitchen. He was peeling an orange. He looked up and smiled at Jessie. There was a little Christmas tree on the kitchen window sill with home-made decorations on it.

"It's all right," said Matthew. "Mum and Dad have gone out. They're doing some last-minute Christmas shopping. So we can talk. Poor Toby must be starving. He can have some of Poppy's cat food. She won't mind. She's a very generous cat." He held out the bowl of oranges to Jessie so she could take one.

"No thank you," she said.

Lucy put three tins of cat food and a tin opener into a rucksack. Matthew rummaged about in a cupboard and found a bowl and a chipped saucer. Then he filled an empty orange-juice bottle with water.

"That's everything we need," said Lucy.

Jessie watched Lucy and Matthew put on their coats and scarves and wellingtons.

"Is that the hut where Toby's going?" asked Jessie as they walked down the back garden.

"Yes," said Matthew. "There's plenty of room for him to sleep, so he should manage, especially as he's not staying long."

Jessie thought, 'He's reminding me of my promise.'

"When are you going to tell, Jessie?" asked Lucy.

"After Christmas," said Jessie.

"When after Christmas?" said Matthew.

Jessie didn't know. She could see Matthew and Lucy turning to look at her as they walked through the deep snow on the field behind their garden.

"Boxing Day," she said suddenly. "That's when I'll tell. Boxing Day."

When they reached the wall which separated the school playground from the field, Jessie said,

"Shall I call Toby? Shall I see if he'll come?"

"Yes," said Lucy. She looked excited, like Jessie did.

"Toby, Toby," called Jessie. She wondered if he'd be able to hear from the bicycle shed. What if the caretaker saw them? What if ... ?

A dark shape appeared in the snow below them. He seemed to be wagging his whole body, not just his tail – he was so pleased to see Jessie. The snow on his coat scattered in all directions.

"Can you climb over the wall, Toby? Can you?" said Jessie.

"Of course you can, Toby," said Matthew.

"Good boy, Toby," said Lucy. She patted the top of the wall with a wet, gloved hand.

He jumped over easily, gracefully, like an athlete. He threw himself on to Jessie, knocking her over in the snow. He licked her face until Lucy and Matthew pulled her up.

Matthew patted Toby.

"I knew you could do it," he said. "I'm sure he's been over lots of times."

Jessie walked next to Toby, stroking his head, knocking the snow off his coat that fell on to him as he walked past the bushes on the field.

"You mustn't be covered in snow when you go in the hut, Toby," she whispered as she bent down to him. "We're taking you to a better place. You'll like it in the hut. It's like a stable."

Snow had blown against the hut window so it let in only a little light. Lucy switched on a battery lamp that was hanging on a nail.

"That's better," said Matthew.

Toby looked round, sniffing, excited, pushing his nose into corners.

"Can we make him a bed?" asked Jessie. "I want him to be comfortable. I want him to like it better than the bicycle shed. He'd only got a coat to sleep on there."

"Did you give him your coat, Jessie?" asked Lucy.

"Is that why you had to borrow one from Lost Property?"

"Yes," said Jessie. "But I swapped it for the lost-property one. I wish I hadn't. It's still there now in the bicycle shed."

"Don't worry, Jessie", said Lucy. "It belonged to Jonathan Bell. He's left now. He left ages ago."

"Oh," said Jessie. "I'm so glad." She saw Matthew putting some old sacks into the bottom of a box. It was a big box, made of wood, and looked as if it would make a good bed for Toby. Lucy was opening a tin of cat food.

There were some bags of hay in a corner of the hut, stored there for Lucy's rabbits which were kept indoors now that it was winter. When Jessie saw them she said, "Do you think Toby could have some hay on top of the sacks? Could you spare some?"

Matthew saw the eagerness in Jessie's face.

"All right," he said. "We've got lots." He took one of the bags and emptied it into the box.

Jessie said, "This is your bed now, Toby. Look, it's like the manger in the stable at Bethlehem."

"There's no donkey, but there might be a mouse or two for company," laughed Matthew.

Later that day Jessie went back to the hut and pinned a gold cut-out star on to the wall above Toby's box with a drawing pin.

Jessie went to bed early that Christmas Eve. It was

nice to think of Toby sleeping in a manger. She would get up early on Christmas morning. As a present she would give him a ball out of the toy cupboard in the kitchen.

After a while, Jessie got out of bed and went over to the window. It was snowing again, but only lightly. 'I wish I could see Lucy and Matthew's garden clearly,' she thought. She could just make out their hut covered in snow and wondered what Toby was doing inside and whether he was sleeping. He'd be comfy on the hay, as comfy as baby Jesus in the stable at Bethlehem. She was glad she had pinned the star on to the wall.

Jessie sat for a long time at the window. She sat until she was too cold to sit there any longer. Mum and Dad were still downstairs. She could hear the television on. She'd have to tell them soon about Toby. 'The day after tomorrow,' thought Jessie. She looked at the luminous fingers on her clock – nearly ten o'clock. She fell asleep soon after but woke again at two. In the darkness she thought she heard a dog bark.

'Is it my dog?' she wondered. 'Is it Toby? Is he barking for me?' thought Jessie.

When she woke again it was morning, not properly light, but she could see the whiteness of the snow through the window. She reached over to the bottom of her bed and felt for her presents.

Yes, there were some. She switched the light on but she didn't feel like opening them yet. She couldn't stop thinking about Toby.

'It's Christmas and he ought to have a proper home,' thought Jessie. 'A hut's not a proper home, even though it's a nice hut. He ought to have proper food. He ought to be taken for a proper walk. He ought to have a warm fire to lie by.'

She opened the door quickly and ran across the landing to her parents' room. She knew she didn't want to keep the secret any longer. She didn't want to wait until Boxing Day to tell them about Toby. If they wouldn't give Toby a proper home, then they'd find someone else who would, even if it meant she couldn't keep Toby herself.

She pushed their door open.

"Mum, Dad," she called. "Can I come in? I've got something to tell you."

A while later, in their home, Lucy and Matthew read a letter that had been put through their letterbox. It said,

Dear Lucy and Matthew,
Toby's not in your hut any longer. I told Mum and Dad early this morning and they let me fetch him. They've said I can keep him if he doesn't belong to anyone and I know he doesn't. Thank you for being my friends and thank you for helping me to look after him. I hope your Christmas is being as happy as mine.

Love from
Jessie

"I'm glad she told," said Matthew.

In her home, Jessie sat on the rug by the fire. A black, brown and white dog lay next to her, his head on his front paws, sleeping. His coat had been brushed almost free of tangles with an old hairbrush.

'I'm glad I told,' she thought. 'I'm glad I told.'

If it hurts, cry

by Christine Laskey

If it hurts, cry

by Christine Laskey

Joe was scared. He had been feeling scared for some time now. He was scared because he knew that soon he would have to do something and he was afraid to do it. He was afraid because he had done it before and it hurt. Sometimes it hurt a bit and sometimes it hurt a lot. It just depended. He had to do it though. It was for his own good. His mother and father and his grandparents had always told him so. These were the people he loved and trusted the most and he knew they loved him very much indeed. He was sure they would never allow anyone to hurt him unless it was absolutely necessary.

Sometimes Joe sat and thought about all the people he had ever known. Most of them were very kind to him and told him what a big, brave boy he was. He did not believe for one minute that any of them would want him to be hurt. There was his teacher, who he liked very much. Then there was the nurse whom called in at school every day to give him his drugs. There was the helper at school who escorted him to the medical room each day and took special care of him whenever he felt too ill to be in class. None of these people would want him to be hurt unless there was a very good reason.

He knew this. But last time it had really hurt a lot and now he was afraid of going back.

Joe knew he had been born with a serious illness. It had a long name that he could not say properly nor remember most of the time. It meant that he had to obey a lot of very important rules. He was never quite sure what would happen if he broke these rules but he knew how important it was to keep them. His parents had told him how important it was. So had his doctor and his teacher.

One of the rules he was forced to obey was that he had to take medicine every day and it was very important not to forget. Another was that he had to keep to a strict and carefully planned diet. His doctor advised his parents about the food he was allowed to eat and how much of anything he should have at any one time. At home, he often watched his parents read the labels on food packets then weigh everything before writing it down and giving it to him. This was called keeping a record of his intake. When occasionally he stayed with his grandparents for the weekend they did exactly the same thing with all his food. At school, he was allowed to eat only what his parents had given him and he had to eat it all or take home what he did not want. Under no circumstances was he allowed to share part of his packed lunch with another child, nor could he share any part of theirs. If one of his friends offered him a cake or a biscuit he had to refuse. Joe knew how important all this was and that his parents and grandparents went to so much trouble because they loved him.

Sometimes, while at home or at school, he might begin to feel sick and dizzy, often losing all sense of what was happening. This was because he was having something called a fit. On these occasions he was given some special, strong medicine by either the school nurse or one of his parents. Afterwards he slept for hours. For this reason he had been told to stay within sight of an adult at all times. This rule was becoming increasingly hard for him to keep as he got older, but it was one which he would never have knowingly broken. He knew the consequences might be very serious if he started to fit and there was no one there to help.

Though he sometimes got fed up with all these rules, he did not mind obeying most of them most of the time. It was the other one he hated. The one about going into hospital for tests every few months. The problem was that some of these tests really hurt. The doctors and nurses, like most other people, were very kind and told him what a big, brave boy he was. He did not believe for one minute they wanted to hurt him but unfortunately they almost always did. They had to do the tests though. He understood this. He knew it was for his own good and so he tried to be brave.

Once in hospital, Joe had to start with a blood test. A nurse or doctor put a needle into his arm and drew blood out with a syringe. The blood sample was then sent to the laboratory for analysis. He might also have a lumbar puncture. For this he had to lie very still while they took some fluid from his spine. Sometimes these tests did not hurt at all, sometimes they hurt a bit and sometimes they hurt a lot. It just depended. The results of this testing helped the doctors to know more about Joe's illness and how his body was managing to cope with it.

He always tried to be grown up during these tests and never cried – even when it really hurt. The doctor was always pleased with him and told him how big and brave he was. Despite this he could not help getting angry inside because doctors did not always tell the truth. On many occasions he had been told that it would not hurt and it had. It was unfair when people did not tell the truth, especially doctors, because then you did not know what to expect. But Joe did not make a fuss because he knew it was not the doctor's fault. The tests had to be done. They were for his own good and he had to be brave.

Now that time was coming again and Joe was so scared he could not even think about it. He tried not to show how frightened he was but somehow his mum and dad seemed to know and they began to worry.

They had explained time and again how they would never let anyone hurt him if it could possibly be avoided, that this was something that had to be done and that they could do nothing to prevent it. Still they were worried and at the next hospital appointment they spoke quietly with the doctor while Joe was with the nurse. They told the doctor Joe was afraid and they were worried because he was becoming increasingly frightened of coming to the hospital ... so frightened he could not even talk about it. The doctor suggested it might be an idea for Joe to see a person at the hospital whose job it was to help children experiencing problems with their treatment.

That night, Joe's parents told him he would be going to see someone at the hospital, not for tests but just to talk. They told him they were beginning to understand that hospitals could get too much for you, especially when you were only eight. This person, who was called a long name which was hard to remember, was there to try to help.

One morning a few weeks later Joe got up but, after washing and dressing, did not go to school as usual. Instead he went to the hospital to see the psychologist. On arrival, he and his mother were taken to the room where she could be found. Upon entering, Joe was very surprised. He had never seen a room like it in a hospital before. It was full of bright, comfortable furniture, lots of lovely books and masses of cuddly toys. The wards and waiting rooms had toys and books in them but those places were not nearly as bright and colourful as this.

The psychologist introduced herself. She was a young, cheerful person with a soft, gentle voice and Joe immediately liked her. She invited him to sit down and he chose a large, comfortable chair where he sat ready to talk. The psychologist, who was called Nicki, suggested that Joe's mother go and get herself some coffee if that was all right with him. Joe said that would be fine and he would see his mother later.

Joe sat patiently and waited for Nicki to talk about the hospital. He thought she would probably talk about his coming check-up and what was going to happen. Instead she asked him what he thought of the playroom. He told her he liked the playroom very much and that the toys and books looked wonderful. Nicki then invited him to play with anything he wanted. He looked round and his eyes rested on a big, cuddly Winnie-the-Pooh. He had read about Pooh Bear in lots of books and had become quite fond of the character. Nicki followed his stare and suggested they play a game with the bear. Joe was a bit surprised but happy to oblige because he did not really want to talk about his coming stay in hospital. He preferred to push that to the back of his mind for as long as possible.

Nicki walked across the room and picked up Winnie-the-Pooh. She handed him to Joe who felt warm and comfortable as he held the bear to him.

"Do you like Pooh?" asked Nicki.

"I've got lots of books about him," Joe told her.

"Pooh isn't well at the moment," said Nicki, smiling warmly. "He's got to go into hospital so they can find out what's wrong with him." Joe looked wide-eyed.

"Will he have to have a blood test?" he asked eagerly.

"Maybe," said Nicki.

" ... and a needle in his back?" continued Joe, who looked sorrowfully at the bear until Nicki interrupted his thoughts.

"Here's a doctor's kit," she said, producing a brightly coloured plastic box. "Perhaps you'd like to be the doctor and examine Pooh."

"Okay," Joe agreed in his most serious tone of voice.

"Good," said Nicki, "I've been really worried about him." She jumped up and walked across the room to a low bed covered with a white sheet and motioned to Joe to place Pooh on it. She then gave him a small white coat to put on.

"Don't worry, Pooh," she said gently, "Doctor Joe is here to take care of you."

"Doctor Hargreaves!" corrected Joe. "I'm Doctor Hargreaves." Doctor Hargreaves was the name of Joe's consultant and he felt that if he were going to take care of Pooh he ought to be a real doctor and do it properly.

"I'm terribly sorry, sir!" Nicki replied apologetically. "Pooh, this is Doctor Hargreaves." Joe examined Pooh carefully, using the stethoscope to listen to his heart and the special little torch to look into his eyes and ears.

"Hmm," he said thoughtfully, 'I think we need to take some blood." Joe looked very serious as he picked up the needle and syringe and pulled back the plunger.

"Now this won't hurt," he told the bear, even though he thought it probably would. He then pushed the needle point heavily into Pooh's arm.

"Ouch!" yelled Nicki's voice. Joe looked up at her.

"That was Pooh," she explained. "I think you must have hurt him."

"You must not shout like that!" Joe addressed Pooh firmly.

"But you hurt him, doctor," protested Nicki. "I think he's going to cry."

"He mustn't," insisted Joe. "He has to be a big, brave bear."

"He is a big, brave bear," Nicki answered gently,

"but I'm afraid he is crying because you hurt him and even big, brave bears cry when something really hurts them."

"But he mustn't cry," persisted Joe. "I have to do it – it's for his own good. I can't help it – it has to be done."

"There's nothing wrong with crying when you are hurt," Nicki persisted in a firm but gentle voice. "Lots of very brave people do."

Joe looked at the floor. Then he carefully put a plaster on the spot where he had taken the blood from Pooh's arm. Just then the door opened and his mum appeared. Nicki smiled at Joe and held out her hand.

"It was lovely to meet you, Joe," she said. "Will you come and play with us again?"

He shook Nicki's hand and smiled.

"Of course," he replied, as the two grown-ups exchanged glances. He and his mum then departed and headed for home.

After that Joe went to see Nicki several times more. Often he played hospitals with the toys and dolls. He also played with the cars or read books and after a while spent a lot of time talking to Nicki. Occasionally, he walked on ahead at hometime leaving one or both of his parents talking to her.

One day, Nicki asked Joe if he would like her to visit him at school and meet his teacher. Joe thought that would be great and told her so. Shortly afterwards, Nicki arrived at Joe's school and he felt very grand as he introduced her to his teacher and all his friends.

In the playroom one day, soon after Nicki's visit to school, she started to talk to Joe about the hospital and how he felt about it. He looked at the floor not wanting to respond. Playing with Nicki and the toys was always such fun he did not want to spoil it.

"You know, Joe," began Nicki, "you'll be coming in soon for a check-up. Are you scared?" Joe did not look up from the floor.

"If I were you," she continued, "I'd be really scared. I bet some of the things the doctors do to you really hurt a lot." Joe looked at her, somewhat surprised. Nobody had ever said anything like that about the hospital before.

"But they have to do it," he said tight-lipped.

"Yes I know," agreed Nicki, "but that doesn't mean you have to like it." Joe made no response to this but stared once again at the floor. "I bet it makes you want to scream and shout," she added. Joe was shocked by her remarks and stared at her in amazement. "But you mustn't cry," he insisted, "you have to be brave."

"Do you?" asked Nicki, eyebrows raised. "Why? I wouldn't. I'd scream."

"But what about the doctors and nurses?" Joe asked. "They'd get cross if you screamed."

"Never mind that," she said. "If I were you I'd be really cross with them!"

"It isn't their fault," said Joe sadly, looking back to the floor. "They have to do it."

"That is true," agreed Nicki, "but it isn't your fault either and I'm sure if your doctor had had to have needles and tests that hurt when he was only six years old he would have cried." Joe sat and clenched his fists. Nicki leaned towards him.

"In fact," she added in a whisper, "he probably still would." Joe tried to smile at her attempt to lighten the atmosphere but his lips tightened and he drew in his breath.

"Doctors do understand that things hurt and make people want to cry you know, Joe," Nicki told him reassuringly.

"Sometimes it really hurts a lot," he managed to say quietly. Tears came to his eyes as he thought about it but he struggled very hard and managed to hold them in. When his dad came to collect him he got up to leave quietly.

"See you next week?" Nicki questioned gently as he walked sadly to the door.

"Yes," he answered quietly and managed to look back with a bit of a smile.

On the way home Joe's Dad talked about the hospital. He, like Nicki, asked Joe if he was scared and said that he understood some of his treatment might be painful and that it must get a bit much for him at times.

When Dad took him to school the next day, he spent a lot of time talking to his teacher. He told her that soon Joe would be going for a short stay in hospital for his regular check-up.

That afternoon when the children were all gathered on the carpet their teacher began to talk to them.

"I've got an idea," she said. "Why don't we set up a hospital corner in the classroom?" It sounded very interesting and they all sat quietly, waiting for further details. "Joe could teach us all about it," she continued, "because he's been in hospital lots of times."

The children were all very enthusiastic and the same day they started to set up their hospital corner next to the home corner. Joe was in charge and felt very important as he arranged along the window-sill the instruments and dishes they had been given by the school nurse .

In the days that followed, as they played in the hospital corner, it made Joe feel good to be able to share his experiences with the other children. It was something he had never had the opportunity to do before. It was also a new and strangely pleasant experience to hear his teacher and other adults talk about how unpleasant hospitals could sometimes be. They had never done this before and so he had always felt that nobody understood. It made him wonder whether they might have known how he had been feeling all along.

When he next visited Nicki, they decided they ought to kick this nasty hospital for all the horrible things it had done to Joe in the past. The two of them walked through the corridors kicking the walls as they went. Joe thought it was a bit silly but it made him feel good. When his parents came to collect him that day they told them what they had been doing.

"Don't forget to kick the hospital on your way out, Joe!" called Nicki as they walked towards the entrance.

"I won't," he called back over his shoulder. On the way out, Joe launched an almighty kick at the wall beside the front entrance. He then looked expectantly towards his mum and dad. They looked helplessly at one another before each kicking the nasty hospital. They looked really funny and it made Joe laugh.

Soon the time came and Joe prepared to be admitted to the hospital. His mum and dad took him one morning with his own small, carefully packed suitcase. As they entered through the big hospital doors, Dad bent down and looked straight into his eyes.

"Don't forget, Joe, this time," he said, "if it hurts, cry." Joe smiled at Dad and took his hand as they walked to the reception desk from where they would be taken up to the children's ward.

A short time later, Joe found himself on a hospital bed with his own consultant and a familiar looking nurse standing beside him.

"I'll try to be quick with this, Joe," said Doctor Hargreaves, "but it might hurt a little bit." That was strange. Doctor Hargreaves had never said anything like that before. Joe held his breath as the needle went into his arm. His mum was holding his other hand. He gasped as it punctured his skin. Then it was over. It was not really bad that time. It happened that way sometimes. Doctor Hargreaves smiled and addressed Joe again.

"We need a little bit more," he told him. "I think we'll take it from your hand this time. Can you hold still for a few more minutes?" Joe nodded.

The nurse held his arm as the doctor pointed the needle towards the back of his hand. As the tip touched his skin he felt a sharp pain. Then suddenly a huge pain shot through his arm making his whole body throb. The next thing he knew, he could hear the loudest scream he had ever heard in his life. He realised with sudden and shocked disbelief that he was listening to himself. He was screaming and crying and yelling at the top of his voice as the hot tears poured down his face. Through all this noise he could hear the reassuring sound of familiar voices.

"It's all right, Joe," they were saying, "it's all right." Then it was all over and he was left with his chest heaving as he breathed in loud, heavy, uncontrolled gasps. His mum and the nurse held him either side as his dad wiped away the tears. Nobody was angry. He had cried and nobody said he was a baby. The only words he could hear were those he must have heard a million times before.

"Good boy, Joe ... brave boy, Joe ... it's over now ... well done, Joe." The same words he had heard before all those times he had held his hurt inside. Then he saw Doctor Hargreaves walking towards him and he was not smiling his usual friendly smile. Joe stiffened. He knew someone would be angry. Someone was bound to be. The doctor stood over Joe with his hands resting on the bed and looked at him. Joe looked back, wide-eyed and horrified at the thought of what the doctor was going to say.

"I'm sorry I hurt you, Joe," he began, "and I want you to know I think you are the bravest little boy I've ever known."

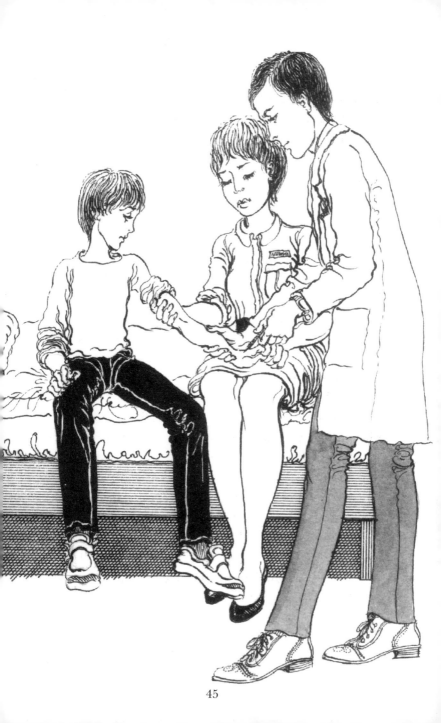

Then he smiled and Joe smiled back. Doctor Hargreaves had called him brave and everyone had said how good he was even though he had screamed and cried.

"Poor Pooh," he said under his breath, "I must have really hurt him. I'm glad he knew he was allowed to cry."

Fans

by John Gordon

Fans

by John Gordon

The pick of Manchester United came trotting down the tunnel on to the pitch. They looked magnificent, but Ginger's dad said, "What a bunch of rubbish!"

"Yeah," said Ginger Biffen. "But here come the boys who are going to stonk 'em."

"Yeah," said his dad.

"Yeah," said Ginger.

Aston Villa, shrugging their shoulders and pretending to be modest, rocked out on to the green.

"Purple dynamite," said Ginger's dad.

Ginger liked it.

"Dynamite!" he said. "Villa are going to blast the wallies off the park."

Jim supported the other side. He kept his head down so he wouldn't catch anyone's eye, and said, "My Man United boys are going to eradicate that lot."

"Eradicate!" Ginger's dad did not have quite as much red hair as his son, but he had a red face to make up for it. "Eradicate! What sort o' stupid word's that?" He saw Jim was embarrassed, so he pushed his shoulder and said "Eh? Eh?" just to make sure he got the point. "What's with eradicate when it's at home?"

Jim kept his eyes on the pitch and mumbled the first words that came into his head.

"It means Man United are going to obliterate 'em – I mean ..." but it was too late.

"Obliter-what!" Ginger's dad laughed: "Hyuck-hyuck-hyuck."

"Leave it off, Dad." Ginger wanted to concentrate on the game. He looked across to where the FA Cup was on display in the stand.

"It's huge," he said to Jim. "Don't it glitter?"

His dad broke in before Jim could reply.

"Told you I was right about the ribbons," he said. The colours of both teams fluttered from the handles. Jim and Ginger had argued about what should be there, but now anyone could see the red and white of United on one side of the cup, and Villa's claret and blue on the other.

"They take the losers' colours off at the end," said Ginger's dad, "and put the winners' ribbons on both sides."

"See?" said Ginger. "That's what I told you."

"Okay, you don't have to rub it in," said Jim.

"We should have asked Dad in the first place because he's a great sportsman."

Jim changed the subject.

"I can't remember who won the toss," he said.

"Jammy Manchester," said Ginger.

"Fix," said the great sportsman and cupped his hands round his mouth to shout down at the referee, "Get on with it, you old fool!"

The referee blew his whistle and Man United passed back.

"Have you ever seen anything like it!" yelled the great sportsman. "They're goin' backwards already!"

It didn't do them any good because a claret shirt streaked through the United front line and whipped the ball off the Manchester player's toes.

"That's the way to do it!" The great sportsman banged Ginger on the back. "He's a good lad." But a moment later the Villa man had lost the ball and United were storming forward.

Flick. Flick. Bam! The Man United striker let loose a cracker that skimmed the turf in a long curve that had the great sportsman groaning all the way as it flew towards the goal.

"No!" he shouted.

"Yes!" yelled Jim, and then ...

feeling very happy!

fantastically excited!

on top of the world! ... he stretched out his arm and reached right down to the pitch to pluck the ball out of the goalmouth.

The Cup Final was in Ginger's bedroom, and they were playing miniature football on the floor beside Ginger's bed.

Jim got the ball out of the net and looked up at Ginger's dad.

"Would you mind getting your foot out of the way, Mr Biffen?" he asked. The big foot was wrinkling the cloth pitch which he and Ginger had spent all morning setting out. The stands and the floodlights were all there, and they had put the cup in its place of honour. The ribbons had been a bit of a problem but they had begged some scraps of material from Ginger's mum, and then they had printed out tickets for the spectators. In the end, Ginger's dad had been the only fan they could manage because the bedroom was not very big.

"Only 50p," Ginger had said when he offered his father a ticket.

"What? You must be joking."

"Royal box," said Ginger. "You always reckon you're something special."

"Royal box!" Mr Biffen was full of scorn. "What do they think they know about football?"

"You could tell 'em," said Ginger. "You could say, 'That round thing's the ball, Your Majesty, and them men with bare knees push it around with their tootsies.' "

Jim had put on a voice full of royal poshness and asked,

"But don't their toes get terribly bent?"

"Yes, Your Majesty," said Ginger, "they've all got

Bent Toe Disease."

"How awful!" squeaked Jim, and they rolled about on the floor until Ginger's dad said, "When you two narners belt up you can share this between you," and he threw a coin on to the pitch.

"A quid," said Ginger. "I told you my dad was a sportsman."

"The greatest," said Jim.

But they'd had to hold up the kick-off until Mr Biffen got back from the pub ...

"I need a bevvy before the big game," he'd said.

At half-time Jim's Manchester were still leading Ginger's Villa one-nil, and Mr Biffen needed more refreshment. He went downstairs to get it from the four-pack he'd brought back from the pub.

"That goal you scored was a fluke, I reckon," said Ginger as they waited for him. "It should be nil-nil."

"That's what your dad says, anyway."

Ginger didn't answer, and they were silent as they helped each other to move the teams to opposite ends. Then Jim said, "He really wants you to win pretty badly, doesn't he?"

"Well, that's what it's all about, ain't it – winning?"

"He thinks so, anyway."

A voice boomed up the stairs,

"Vi-lla! Vi-lla! Stuff United!" and the great sportsman barged into the room and became the crowd. He breathed smoke over the pitch.

"Dad!" Ginger complained. "I'll have to put the floodlights on in a minute."

"Atmosphere," said his father. "You got to get the big match atmosphere," and he started to sing, "Why are we waiting? Why are we rotten well waiting ... ?"

It was Jim's turn to blow the whistle, and Ginger kicked off. The ball rattled off one of Jim's men and ran into touch.

"Villa ball!" yelled the great sportsman. When Ginger put the ball on the touchline ready for the throw-in, his father said, "Pinch a yard, man! Pinch a yard. That's what it's all about."

Ginger did so, but Jim wasn't having any.

"You got to go back and take it again," he said.

"Get out!" Ginger's dad was disgusted. "Give the lad a chance." But Jim put the ball back on the spot where it had crossed the line, and Ginger took the throw quickly without arguing.

The ball was stabbed swiftly from little man to little man.

"Get stuck in!" yelled the crowd as a Villa player sent a red shirt sprawling. "Give 'em a bit o' stick!"

"Foul!" Jim blew the whistle.

"He dived!" roared the crowd. "Play on!" and Ginger's finger gave a quick flick. A claret shirt went twirling up the pitch, tickled the ball forward and dribbled it into the corner of the Manchester net.

"Goal!" The crowd went wild, and Jim looked over the roof of the main stand where the face of Ginger's dad filled the sky like God.

"I was fouled," said Jim.

"Not on your Nellie," said God.

"It wasn't a proper goal."

God lifted his hand and thrust a finger into the sky.

"Number one!" he chanted. "Easy! Easy!"

It was as useless as arguing with a thunder cloud, and while it was going on Ginger had got all his players back into his own half. So Jim made the best of it and kicked off for the restart.

One-one. Cigarette smoke lay in blue layers across the room, and play became very hot. Ginger and Jim were both dab hands at flick and dash. They got better, thrusting the little players forward to curve around opponents, taking the ball forward at the same time, then breaking free for some great solo runs. There were long throw-ins and clever corner kicks that had the goalkeepers diving at full stretch, and the room rocked to the roar of the crowd.

But no goals came.

Then Ginger, attempting an elaborate chip over a crowd of players in front of goal, injured himself.

"I've damaged me flick-finger!" he cried.

Jim blew up to stop play.

"I'll send on the trainer," he said, and he made Ginger hold out his finger to be massaged. "Is it a calf muscle?" he asked as he rubbed.

Ginger winced. "It's a ligament, I reckon."

"A what-a-ment?" said his father.

"Or maybe a hamstring," Ginger groaned.

"Try it out," said Jim, and Ginger's finger limped slowly over the turf.

"Come here," Jim called him back, spat on his own finger and rubbed Ginger's knuckle. "Magic sponge," he said. "You're okay now," and Ginger's finger hopped around like an Olympic pole-vaulter.

Ginger's dad looked up at the ceiling.

"Kids!" He clicked his tongue. "Tch-tch. They don't take nothing seriously."

But the game hotted up even more. They swung the ball about so expertly that the great sportsman bent closer and closer until he was looming right over the pitch. Great wafts of smoke and beer heated the back of Jim's neck as the crowd, very one-sided, yelled Villa on. In spite of that, Manchester held their own.

Then came disaster ... for Manchester.

Ginger's Villa, starting from well within their own half, came rampaging down the pitch, sliced through the defence with a great one-two that left Jim standing, and fired. The shot missed, and Jim's

defender came in with a sliding tackle that up-
ended the Villa striker and left him face down in
front of goal.

"Ref-er-ee!" bellowed the crowd, and Ginger
pointed to the penalty spot.

There could be no doubt about it. It was a foul.
Worse. Jim glanced down at the watch they had laid
at the corner of the pitch and saw they were in the
last minute of time.

"Give me the whistle," said the great sportsman.
"I'll blow for the kick."

The players were cleared from in front of goal
and made to stand at the edge of the penalty box.
Ginger picked up the ball, made sure it was placed
precisely on the spot, and selected his man for the
kick.

Jim had a keeper with his arms up as if already
tipping a ball over the bar, and he put him in the
goalmouth and grasped the control rod behind the
net.

"Get him back," said the great sportsman, and
nudged the keeper with a thick finger. "He's got to
be on the line. And don't move."

Ginger and Jim sized each other up.
They knew the rules, the goalkeeper had to be
motionless until the ball was struck.

"Are you ready, Manchester?"

Jim nodded.

"Are you ready, Villa?"

Ginger nodded, and his father blew a blast on the whistle that made them deaf.

Ginger's man dashed forward and slammed the ball with all his power. Jim didn't have a chance. His muscles seemed to freeze and he squinted as though the ball was heading straight for his own face – but it was the keeper it struck, full force.

"Saved!" Jim yelled. "Great save!"

At that moment two things happened. The watch timer began to peep-peep and the ball went bounding down the pitch, heading straight for Ginger's goal.

Ginger flung himself full length along his bedroom floor to get to his keeper. Too late. His hand had just reached the control rod when the ball, with its final roll, trickled over the line.

"Is it there?" Jim leant forward.

"Yeah," said Ginger. He put his hands to his head and fell back as Jim leapt to his feet.

"I've won the cup! I've won the cup!"

Jim was still dancing when the great sportsman spoke.

"Hold on a minute," he said. "What you getting so excited about?"

"I've just won the cup, that's what," said Jim, and he watched Ginger lift it from the stand for the presentation ceremony.

"Tough luck, Ginge," said Jim.

Ginger managed to grin.

"Great game, though," he said, and held out the cup.

"What's got into you two?" Ginger's dad was indignant. "That ball never got into the net before the final whistle."

"Well you didn't blow," said Ginger, "so I thought we was in injury time."

"Rubbish!"

"He's right, Mr Biffen," said Jim. "There was a hold-up for Ginger's finger, don't forget."

"You got to admit it, Dad," said Ginger. "Jim won."

Silence. The great sportsman looked from one to the other. The eyes in his red face had tightened to tiny blue whirlpools. Suddenly he took a deep breath, reached forward, snatched the cup from Jim's hand and hurled it across the room.

Its lid came off and landed softly on Ginger's bed, but the rest of the cup smashed into the wall and split into silver fragments that fell to the floor with ribbons fluttering.

"Stupid kids' game!" the great sportsman's foot rucked up the edge of the pitch. All the players tottered and some of them fell flat as he slammed out of the room.

They heard his feet thud in the hall before either of them spoke.

"Pitch invasion," said Jim.

It was a feeble joke but Ginger, who had gone pale, managed a thin, little smile.

"It's always the fans who cause the trouble," he said.

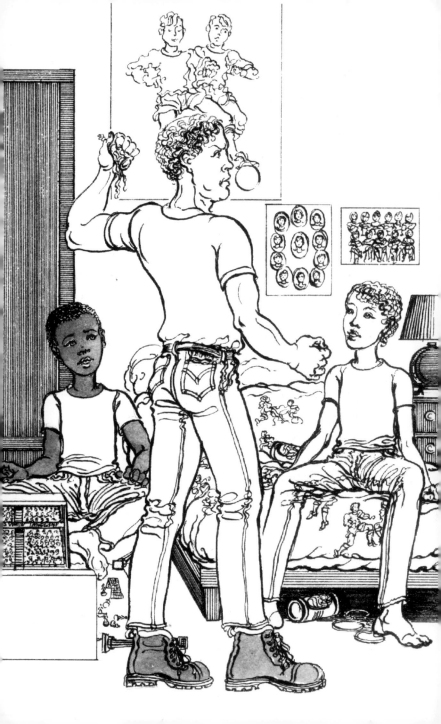

Erin's room

by Stan Cullimore

Erin's room

by Stan Cullimore

"Erin?" Dad poked his head round the door and looked into the bedroom, where his daughter was sitting up in bed reading.

"Hi, Dad – are you coming in?"

Dad pushed the door open and stood in the doorway, with a smile on his face.

"I'd love to come in. The question is – how?"

Erin put down her book and frowned.

"What do you mean – how?"

"I mean – how do I get into your room? It's full of junk."

Erin sighed. "No, it isn't."

Dad put his hands on his hips.

"I don't wish to sound like something out of a pantomime, young lady, but, yes it is!"

"No, it isn't!"

"Yes, it is," said Dad cheerfully.

Erin sighed again.

"If you must know, father. It isn't junk," she spread her arms. "These are my belongings."

Dad threw back his head and roared with laughter.

"I might have known that you would have a fancy name for it." He stepped over a pile of dirty rugby kit, and sat on the edge of the bed. "So tell me. What exactly is the difference between junk, and belongings?"

Erin shook her head.

"There's no point in trying to tell you Dad. You wouldn't understand."

Dad moved a plate covered in toast crumbs and sat further back on to the bed. He nodded.

"I expect you're right – tell me something. Would Mum understand?"

Erin groaned.

"Of course not. Mum doesn't understand anything about my bedroom. She keeps asking me to tidy it up!"

Dad pretended to look horrified.

"What? Tidy up your room – that's unthinkable! Why, if you had a tidy room you might actually be able to walk into it without stepping over something that smells."

Erin rolled her eyes – her father was off on one of his little speeches.

"I mean," continued Dad. "If you had a tidy room, you might actually be able to find things – and not just lose them."

"What do you mean – lose things? I know exactly where every single one of my belongings is, actually, Dad." Erin picked up her book. "So there!"

Dad grinned.

"Rubbish," he said. "Anyway, I didn't come up here to moan about the disgusting state of your room."

"Good." Erin put down the book again. "Then why did you come up to my room, Dad?"

"Because I haven't seen you since this morning. I wanted to find out what your day was like."

Erin looked suspicious.

"What do you mean – what was my day like? I was at school."

Dad nodded. "I know."

"So it was boring, obviously. That's the whole point of school, Dad. It's a punishment for being young."

Dad frowned.

"Is it? I rather enjoyed being at school myself."

"But, Dad – you were weird. In fact, you still are!"

Dad tried to look hurt.

"No, I'm not."

Erin sighed.

"Dad – you write books. Of course you're weird."

"Oh," Dad nodded. "Silly me, I forgot."

He decided it was time to change the subject.

"So," he said. "What about tomorrow? Is that going to be equally as boring as today?"

Erin shook her head, sadly.

"No," she replied. "It's going to be much worse. I've got English."

"English. What's wrong with English?" asked Dad. "It used to be your favourite subject, apart from drama."

"Not any more. I've got a new English teacher, Mister Stubbs, and he's a pain. He always makes you do stupid things. And if you don't do them properly, he gives you a detention."

"What sort of stupid things?"

"Poetry readings!" groaned Erin. "And storytelling." She snorted. "And you'll never guess what we've got to do tomorrow!" She pulled a face. "We've got to read out a poem or story that we've written."

Dad looked puzzled.

"But that sounds like fun!"

Erin rolled her eyes.

"We've got to do it in front of the whole class, Dad. It'll be so embarrassing. And what's worse, Mister Stubbs has invited one of his friends to come and watch us."

"What's wrong with that?"

"She's going to give out a prize for the best one!"

Dad looked even more puzzled.

"But that sounds good, you might win something. You're always telling me that you want to be an actress. Well, here's a chance to stand up in front of an audience – and actually get a prize for doing it."

"You just don't understand, Dad. Knowing Mister Stubbs, his friend is bound to be really pathetic. So is the prize."

Dad looked thoughtful. It was time to change the subject again.

"So," he said. "What story are you going to read out, then?"

Erin lay down.

"One I wrote last week, about a dog that can talk."

"Can I have a look at it? I might be able to think of some ideas to help you with it."

Erin yawned.

"Thanks for the offer, Dad. But I've left it at school in my locker. Sorry."

Dad stood up.

"That's all right, love." He bent down and kissed her on the forehead. "Anyway, goodnight."

Erin rolled over.

"Goodnight, Dad."

The next morning at seven fifteen, Mum walked into Erin's room.

"Erin, time to get up."

She stopped and looked round at the piles of clothes strewn all over the floor. Then she looked at the heaps of books that were dripping off the desk.

She put her hands on her hips.

"Erin Griffiths, this room is a disgrace."

Erin sat up in bed and yawned.

"Morning, Mum."

"Don't you 'morning Mum' me," replied her mother. "This room is a tip. I wouldn't ask a pig to live here."

Erin climbed out of bed and stretched.

"Good," she said. "I wouldn't want to share my room with a pig, anyway."

Her mother glared at her.

"It's no good trying to be funny. When you come home from school today, I want this room tidied up. Do you understand?"

Erin nodded.

When her mother was annoyed, the best thing to do was to agree with her.

"I mean," continued Mum, "can you give me one good reason why you have to make such a mess?"

There was silence for a few seconds while Erin tried to think of one. But sadly, she couldn't.

"I thought not," said Mum. "Well, until you can think of one good reason why you have to make such a mess, I expect this room to remain tidy. Now hurry up and get dressed, you'll be late for school."

At one thirty that afternoon, Dad was sitting at his word processor when the telephone on his desk began to ring he sighed and picked it up – he hated being interrupted.

"Dad?"

"Hello, Erin. How can I help you?"

"I'm in trouble."

Dad nodded.

"What's new?"

"No, honestly, I am. I've got English after lunch and I can't find my locker key."

"So?"

Erin sighed.

"If I can't find my locker key, I can't get my story out of my locker, can I?"

"So?" said Dad, who wasn't really concentrating.

"Dad, if I can't get my story out of my locker, then I can't read it out to the class, can I? And Mister Stubbs will kill me!"

"Oh," Dad nodded. "Now I understand. You need to find your locker key, don't you?"

"Dad," said Erin sarcastically. "You're a genius."

Her father ignored her.

"So, the question is – where did you lose it?"

"I haven't lost it, it's in my bedroom."

Dad stood up.

"All right. I tell you what, I'm on the wander phone. I'll just nip up to your room – you can tell me where the key is. Then I'll bring it up to school for you." He began to walk up the stairs.

"Thanks, Dad," said Erin, gratefully.

Seconds later there was a gasp down the line.

"Dad? Are you all right?" asked Erin nervously.

"I am. But your room isn't. I'd forgotten what a tip it is," groaned Dad.

Five minutes later, two things had happened. One, Dad had searched as much of the room as he possibly could, and two, Erin had run out of money to put into the telephone.

"It's no good," sighed Dad. "I'm never going to find it in all this mess. I'm sorry, Erin. I'm afraid you're just going to have to explain the situation to Mister Stubbs and hope that he lets you off."

"No chance!" muttered Erin. "You don't know what he's like."

"Well then," said Dad, "why don't you just tell your story about the talking dog from memory."

"Because I've forgotten it," snapped Erin.

"In that case, make up another one."

"What about?"

Dad shrugged.

"I don't know. Think of something that has happened to you recently, and make up a story about it."

"Like what?" asked Erin.

Before Dad could reply, the money ran out for the telephone – and the line went dead.

At four o'clock that same afternoon, when Mum and Dad were in the kitchen having a cup of tea, the front doorbell rang.

"I expect that'll be Erin," said Dad, standing up. "I wonder how she got on with her English story."

"Not very well, I expect," said Mum. "But it's her own fault. That's what happens if you don't tidy your room – you lose things." She also stood up. "Hopefully, her experience with the locker key will have taught her a lesson!"

"I doubt it," said Dad. "Anyway, I'll go and let her in." He walked down the hallway.

Sure enough, it was Erin.

"Well," said Dad. "How did it go?"

By way of an answer, Erin threw down her schoolbag and leapt at her father. Then she flung her arms around his neck and gave him a hug.

"Dad," she cried. "You're a genius!"

Over her shoulder, Dad smiled at Mum.

"So," he said, after Erin had let go of him, "obviously it didn't go that badly, after all."

"Badly?" echoed Erin. "It went brilliantly! I came top of the class – and I got the part."

Dad looked puzzled.

"I beg your pardon?"

Erin grinned.

"I got the part."

Her mother and father exchanged glances.

"What part?" asked Mum.

"And it's all thanks to you, Dad, and you, Mum."

Erin stretched out her arms and began to whirl around the hallway with excitement. Her mother and father exchanged glances again. They were both very confused.

"What on earth are you talking about, Erin?" asked Mum.

"Yes, tell us what happened – from the beginning," added Dad. "We're both confused."

Erin shivered happily.

"Well," she said, sitting on the bottom stair. "It all began after I had phoned Dad. He told me that I should tell a story in English, about something that had happened to me. So I did."

"And?" asked Dad.

"Well, everyone agreed that it was the best story they had heard for ages. Especially Mister Stubbs' friend – she thought it was 'really well observed'."

"Oh, that is good," said Dad, proudly.

"There's more," cried Erin. "She said that since I had told the best story, she had something to ask me ..."

"What was it?" asked Mum.

"She asked if I would like to appear in a programme on television."

"What?" gasped Mum and Dad together. "On television?"

"Yes," nodded Erin. "She's a television producer. That's why she came along to watch us. She was looking for a child to appear in her latest TV show.

It's got to be someone who is good at making up stories ... and she wants me to do it!"

"That's excellent!" cried Dad. "Well done, Erin. I'm proud of you."

"She says she's going to give you a ring and make sure it's all right with both of you before she does anything else."

"Of course it is," said Dad. "Isn't it, dear?"

Mum nodded.

"Of course it is."

They were all silent for a few seconds as the news sank in.

"So, what's for tea, then?" asked Erin.

"I don't know – what do famous actresses usually have for tea, dear?" said Dad, turning to smile at Mum.

Mum smiled back.

"I haven't got a clue," she said. "But I do know one thing about famous actresses, they don't get any tea until their rooms are tidy."

Erin giggled.

"Oh dear. That means I'll never get any tea."

"Why not?" asked Dad.

"Because Mum told me that I didn't have to tidy my room if I could think of one good reason why it didn't need to be tidy. Didn't you, Mum?"

Mum nodded.

"Yes, I did."

"Well, now I've found a good reason," said Erin happily.

"Have you, indeed?" asked Mum.

"Yes."

"What is it then?"

"My story."

"Which reminds me, Erin," whispered Dad. "Can you tell me this story of yours? I might be able to use it in one of my books."

"One thing at a time, love," said Mum. "I want to hear this 'reason to be messy', before I hear the story."

"Don't worry, Mum," said Erin. "They're both the same. You see, the story I told was about this girl who had a really messy room and a mum who said that unless the girl could think of a good reason to keep her room messy she had to tidy it up."

"Sounds familiar," said Mum.

"Yep," agreed Erin. "Then, one day, this girl left her homework story in her locker, and left her locker key in her bedroom. Her Dad couldn't find it because of all the mess so the girl had to make up a new story. And because it was such a good story – she came top of the class."

"I don't understand this," muttered Dad.

"Well, you see," said Erin. "This girl's mum always wanted her to come top of the class ..."

Mum nodded. "That's true."

"And the only reason that she came top was because of the story she told."

"I still don't understand," muttered Dad.

"And the only reason she could tell such a good story was because she had lost her locker key in her messy bedroom ..."

Dad frowned.

"In other words," said Erin, happily, "having a messy room makes you come top of the class – which is a very good reason to leave your room messy, isn't it, Mum?"

"Yes," sighed Mum. "I suppose so." She shook her head. "Honestly – I don't know where you get your ideas from, Erin."

"Nor do I," said Dad. "But I tell you what – I like that story. I'm going to use it in one of my books, one day.

Do you know what? He did use the story in a book. And you've just read it!

A death in the family

by Moira Andrew

A death in the family

by Moira Andrew

Sunday

Woke up to hear the telephone ringing in the middle of the night – the middle of the night! Nobody calls at this time just to chat. Ducked under the covers.

Noises of Dad stumbling downstairs. Mum whispering, "Who on earth can it be?"

Then it all happened in slow motion. Dad mumbled our number, said, "Oh no," in a pushing-things-away kind of voice and we all listened, hardly breathing. Mum, my brother, me. The hall clock boomed out three o'clock and the sound echoed across the darkness.

Mum said quietly, "It's Mum, isn't it?"

And it was – is. I can't believe it. Grandma is dead.

Just yesterday she was out shopping in her favourite blue-check jacket, buying custard powder, cat food, toilet paper, baked beans, chocolate for me (a Saturday treat) and mint sweets for my brother (not that he deserves them!)

Now she won't go into the supermarket ever again – or anywhere. I wonder where she's gone?

Couldn't get back to sleep, so decided to write

about it. Writing helps, especially when nobody comes along to check your spelling and things.

I've never known anyone who has died before. Lucy doesn't count, because she was a hamster, but I remember that she looked as though she was still sleeping. I wonder if that's how Grandma looks.

Now Mum's calling up the stairs. Breakfast – breakfast on a day like this! I'm not hungry.

Later

Went to visit Grandad. He hadn't shaved and had white prickles all over his chin. It made him look different. He wasn't exactly crying, but he sounded croaky.

Nobody seemed to remember where the tea is kept, so I put the kettle on and made tea for everyone – except Steve, of course. He was outside kicking stones about the garden. Brothers! Worse than useless!

When I gave Mum her mug of tea she really looked at me for the first time. She hugged me and said, "You're a good girl, Sophie. Grandma would have been proud of you." That made me feel very sad inside.

It was funny in a way. All morning I half-expected to hear Grandma's voice, "Sophie Girl," (she always calls me that.) "Come on up and give your old granny a kiss! Let's look through my earring box and find a pair to match your T-shirt."

Grandma and I could spend hours trying on earrings – shiny ones, jewelled ones, long silver ones, earrings for parties, earrings for going shopping, earrings to startle the neighbours! Grandma loves – loved – earrings and so do I.

Mum said Grandad had better think about getting shaved and dressed. She said that the undertakers would soon be on their way.

"Undertakers" has a horrible sound, like the end of the world. Makes me shiver.

Grandad went upstairs ever so slowly. He opened the bedroom door and went inside. I wondered about Grandma lying there under her pink flowery duvet cover. She bought it in a sale not so long ago. She said it made the bedroom look like a photograph she had seen in *Homes and Gardens*.

Steve wouldn't come into the house. He said it was creepy and Mum said no, it was just the same as yesterday. So Dad said, "Leave the boy alone, Sally. He'll come to it in his own time." I took him out a biscuit and a can of lemonade and he didn't even say thank you.

Went home in the car with Dad. Mum stayed with Grandad. They came back at teatime and brought some little cakes Grandma baked yesterday. Yesterday – seems like ages ago! I couldn't eat them, but old Greedy-guts Steve had four!

Monday

School as usual. I couldn't believe that assembly and maths and swimming went on as though nothing had happened. Everybody was going on about watching telly, going round town with their parents, awful aunties coming to Sunday tea. Polly said I was a bit quiet. She asked about my weekend and I had to tell her about Grandma.

"Did you see her?" Polly asked. "What did she look like?"

I said I didn't want to talk about it and Polly said she was sorry she'd asked and had just wanted to show a bit of interest and didn't really care and didn't expect her best friend to go off in a huff.

So I said I was sorry and we were friends again, but we didn't say any more about Grandma.

Then Mr Watson asked me to come out to his desk and he said he was sorry to hear about my grandmother, so Polly must have told him. Everybody seems to be sorry about something today.

"Try not to be too upset, Sophie," Mr Watson said. "Your grandmother was getting on (He meant she was old!) and she's had a good life. We all have to go sometime."

What does he know? Grandma wasn't old – well, not to me. And I bet she didn't want to "go"! She wanted to stay around and read her books and go shopping and have her hair done and look after her garden and things. Why did she buy lots of bulbs for next spring if she wanted to "go"? Mr Watson made me so furious that I felt like crying. But I didn't. Everyone would have made a fuss and how I feel about Grandma is private!

Teatime started off quietly. Mum looked kind of streaky about the eyes, so I think she'd been crying quite a lot. She wasn't at work today, but Dad went to work as usual. Then Steve told a couple of his silly jokes, but Dad shut him up and sent him to his room. Mum said it wasn't fair. Steve stamped off upstairs and turned his record player on full blast. I thought Dad would shout at him again, but he didn't. Everything seems upside down today.

Went to see Grandad later. He was watching the telly with old Roxy purring away like a steam engine on his knee. Grandad was just like he always is, but it was very odd with Grandma's chair empty and no "Come in, Sophie Girl and give me a kiss."

The cake tins were empty too, so we had chocolate biscuits instead. Unheard of when Grandma's around!

Went upstairs and peeped round Grandma's bedroom door. It looked just as usual with her pink dressing gown over the chair. There was still a touch of Grandma's perfume, but they'd taken her away and everything was quiet and tidy.

"Too tidy," I thought.

I tiptoed in to look in Grandma's earring box. I got out her best crystal ones and put them on. They winked in the mirror like little stars and I remembered Grandma saying they were for "high days and holidays". For a minute I thought I heard her voice, but no – I won't ever hear it again.

Then I started to cry. I cried and cried and I couldn't stop.

Mum came up and found me.

"Sophie's had enough," she said. I sniffled and snuffled all the way home and I didn't think I'd sleep. But I did.

Tuesday

School wasn't so bad today. We had a supply teacher and she brought piles of interesting workcards. She let us use our felt tips after we had finished our writing. Then we stood at the gate and did a traffic survey. We had clipboards and coloured pens and ticked boxes to find out how many cars and lorries and bikes went past between break and lunchtime.

I almost forgot about Grandma until one of those big black funeral cars went by.

"Where do we put a hearse, Mrs Scott?" Polly asked. Then she clapped her hand over her mouth. "Oh, Sophie, I didn't think," she said. We decided to put the hearse in the miscellaneous box, but I felt my heart squeeze up like a handkerchief with a knot in it.

At afternoon break Polly said, "Do you know when your Grandma's funeral is?"

"No, I don't," I said, pushing the whole idea out of my mind. Polly looked as though she was going to say something else, but she didn't. Then the bell went.

Mrs Scott read to us until hometime. It was a really funny book and had us all in fits of laughter. I had thought I'd never laugh again!

Grandad came to tea. He said that Roxy is moping and off her food. She only seems happy when she lies on his knee. I expect Roxy misses Grandma too.

Afterwards Steve and I were shooed off to watch television or read or something as the grown-ups had "matters to discuss". About Grandma, I suppose. Aunts and uncles and cousins arrived and they all had drinks and coffee downstairs. Sometimes you'd think Grandma had nothing to do with me the way they go on.

Felt quite cross, so I decided to write up my diary. Grandma always said writing was a good way of making sense of things.

Wednesday

Steve made a fuss about going to school this morning. Mum said it wasn't like him and Steve said nothing was like itself at the moment. Mum said, "Too bad," and he'd just have to live with it and did he want cheese or cold ham in his sandwiches.

Had Mrs Scott again today. She makes everything really interesting and I wish we had her all the time. Mr Watson is away on a course and is coming back tomorrow.

Polly said she'd seen a notice about Grandma in the papers. It said she was the "beloved grandmother of Steven and Sophie". Polly was a bit jealous. She's never had her name in the paper.

"What's it like to be famous?" she asked.

I said I didn't know but if it meant Grandma dying to make you famous I'd rather not. (Must have a look at the paper when I get home!)

Mum and Dad told us that Grandma's funeral is to be on Friday, so Steve and I won't be going to school. Mum fussed about seeing what clothes we had to wear. She said we had to look respectable and that Steve must wear a tie. He gave Mum one of his special black-cloud looks, but he didn't say anything.

The telephone kept ringing all evening and I heard Dad telling people about the "arrangements" over and over again.

Went to bed early, but I couldn't get to sleep. I kept thinking about Grandma being cold and lonely. Mum heard me crying and brought me a mug of hot chocolate. We talked about Grandma for a long time and Mum told me about when she was a little girl. Then she got out some old photographs and we laughed at Grandma in a mini-skirt and Grandad in long shorts and Mum squinting up at the sun in her little sun-bonnet.

Must have gone to sleep at last because I don't remember any more.

Thursday

Mr Watson was back today and as boring as ever. Gave him a note about tomorrow and he put on his caring crow look which he keeps for special occasions like this. Saw grey hairs sprouting out of his ears and wondered how Mrs Watson stands him.

He forgot about being caring when I got my maths wrong.

"Sophie Collins," he yelled. "Don't you ever listen to anything I say? Daydreaming again, I suppose." So I said, "Sorry Mr Watson. I was thinking about something else." Then he must have remembered about Grandma because he just said,

"Well then, you'd better have another go and try to use your brains this time!"

Polly asked what the funeral was going to be like

and I said, "How do I know? I've never been to one before," and she said, "Keep you hair on, I only asked!"

I told Polly that there was to be a kind of party at our house after Grandma's funeral was over and she said was I sure, because it sounded a funny idea to her. I thought it was funny too, but Mum and Dad said that it is the proper thing to do.

Grandad came to tea again. He said he must get out of the habit and begin to look after himself again and Mum said, "Okay, Dad. Next week you're on your own."

It sounded so sad that we all just looked down at our plates and you could hear everybody chewing. Then Mum and Dad both started to say something at the same time and that made us all laugh.

Dad took Grandad home. When I kissed him goodnight Grandad said, "It will be better once all this is over, Sophie Girl, I promise you."

Grandad never called me Sophie Girl before.

Friday

Woke up early. The sky is still pale pink and the sun is just a gold band across the sky. It's the day nobody wanted to happen – the day we say goodbye to Grandma for ever. I don't think I can bear it. Got out my diary to help me think.

Later

We all had a late breakfast and even Steve had no jokes and made no fuss about which cereal to have. When Mum went into the kitchen Dad said, "Look after your mum today, kids. She's going to find it hard going."

So Steve and I did the washing up and Dad whizzed about with polish and duster. "All the relations are coming back here afterwards," he said. "Can't let the side down."

Went out and mooched around in the garden. It was still bright with flowers. "Grandma would have loved this," I thought. Then I picked loads of asters, pink and blue and purple. I raided the dahlia bed, cut the few carnations left and anything else still in bloom, my bunch of flowers growing by the minute.

Mum said, "Sophie, what on earth are you doing?"

"They're for Grandma," I said, so Mum didn't go on. She knew all about Grandma and her flowers. The whole family used to laugh at her, flowers everywhere.

"Can't get away from them even in the loo," Grandad used to grumble.

I tied my flowers with a ribbon and put a note to Grandma in my best writing. A poem would have been better, but I hadn't time to write one.

We got dressed in our best things, (nothing black

except Dad's tie) but I had to wear a skirt (which I hate) and Steve had to wear his school tie (which he hates). Nobody made a fuss.

We went to Grandad's and there were lots of cars outside. Then we all went inside and said a prayer. It didn't seem real – more like a film on television. I kept thinking that the only person missing all this was Grandma!

Next we went back into the cars and all followed the hearse. I didn't want to think about Grandma lying there all alone in a box under loads of flowers, so I looked out of the window and counted the lampposts. I got to 203 and then we got to the crematorium – another awful word. Can't they think of anything nicer?

Mum said to put my bunch of flowers on Grandma's coffin.

"These are for you, Grandma," I whispered and then I said, "Thank you, Sophie Girl," because Grandma would have said it if she could.

People had lots of nice things to say about Grandma. It would have made her laugh, I expect. We sang some hymns and listened to music and Dad read a poem that Grandma specially liked. It was about friends and fountains by Brian Somebody.

The best bit went like this, "And a fountain empties itself into the grass." I was so busy saying it over and over to myself that I missed Grandma's coffin disappearing behind some purple velvet curtains. I looked up and it had gone – so soon – with my grandma shut away inside.

Then it was all over and we were outside in the sunshine again, admiring all the flowers people had sent. Mum cried a bit and some of the relatives had their hankies out, but it wasn't as bad as I had expected.

When we went home we had this kind of party and we met cousins and aunties we hardly knew. Steve squirmed and looked like thunder when they said, "What a big boy you are!" and things like that. He disappeared into the garden and I went to help in the kitchen.

Found one of the uncles in the kitchen drinking port or something and making silly jokes and laughing like a drain. That made me mad.

"It's my Grandma's funeral!" I said. "Not a Christmas party!" He stopped laughing and looked a bit put out.

"Sorry, Sophie. I didn't think," he said.

Grandad wouldn't stay. He said he had to go home to feed the cat, but I think he just wanted to be on his own.

Afterwards when we were clearing up Mum said, "It's the end of an era," and she sighed. Wasn't quite sure what an era was, so I looked it up in the dictionary later. It means "a series of years reckoned from a particular point" – a good word. Must use it in a poem and give Mr Watson something to think about!

Had time to write a bit before I went to bed.

Big question, Where is Grandma now? I wonder if she can see what's happening. I wish I knew.

Saturday

A Saturday like any other – almost. No treats from Grandma, of course, but we went to town in the morning, played on our bikes in the afternoon and watched telly before we went to bed.

Sunday

A whole week since Grandma died. It seems like months.

Grandad came to Sunday lunch. He brought flowers from the garden for Mum, a £10 note for Steve and a parcel for me.

"That's from your grandma," he said. I felt all round the parcel with my fingers.

"Aren't you going to open it?" asked Mum.

I guessed what was inside and didn't want to open it when everybody was looking, so I went up to my room.

It was Grandma's earring box. I spilled all the earrings on to the floor in a great, sparkling heap – shiny ones, pearl ones, long silver ones, earrings shaped like cats, tiny golden ones and the special crystal ones for "high days and holidays".

I couldn't wait to show Polly, so I phoned to ask her round after lunch. We spent the whole afternoon trying on one pair of earrings after another. We pranced about admiring ourselves in the dressing-table mirror.

I wondered if Grandma was watching. I imagined her saying, "Now those earrings look a treat, Sophie Girl!"

Polly saw me smiling to myself.

"What are you grinning at?" she asked.

"Nothing much," I said. "I was just thinking about Grandma."

The good guy

by Jan Needle

The good guy

by Jan Needle

Matthew was the cleverest boy in the school. Everybody knew it, there was no doubt – himself, his Mum and Dad, the teachers and all the other kids. There was just no contest. He was top of the class in everything. The only thing he didn't like about school was the fact that there weren't really classes as such to be top of. Despite the sort of area it was in, despite the fact that most of the kids were hopeless and half of them could hardly even speak English, they were quite progressive and modern in the way they taught – the teachers said so constantly. Instead of classes, they had things called family units, with kids of every age and ability mixed in together. But even though Matthew couldn't come out top, everyone knew he was the best.

Although Matthew liked the feeling, he was never cocky about it. He wandered around the family unit modestly, helping people out with a sum here, or the spelling of a word there. All the teachers liked him – he was clean, neat and well-behaved as well as being clever, but he never acted like a teacher's pet. He was good at lessons, but he was good at sport as well – and games, and rough and tumbles in the playground. He mixed in with the other kids. He didn't try to set himself up as being better. He was a good guy.

It was always assumed – and the Headmistress had even said it at prize giving – that Matthew would do well in everything. When he had finished in the juniors he would go to the best comprehensive in the smarter part of town. After that he would take his A-levels – and pass them, lots of them. Then go to university. He often wondered what he would study there, because he couldn't make up his mind. He rather fancied becoming a famous scientist a lot of the time. But perhaps it would be more fun to be an actor. He'd get on television and everyone would stare at him in the street. He had years to make up his mind, so there was no hurry.

Matthew thought that the other kids were a different kettle of fish. The school was in an area with high unemployment and a population that changed almost constantly, as parents moved from place to place. It was on the outskirts of a huge city and there were many children in the school of different races. Most of them could speak English, although many of them were better in the language their parents spoke; but a few could hardly speak English at all. Nimraj was like that. She could understand a lot and she could answer with a few words.

Nimraj was one of seven children and the family lived in a tumbledown terrace house in the roughest part of the area. Her father had been killed in an accident the year before. All the family looked the same – thin, miserable and sometimes dirty. To make matters worse for Nimraj, she had a cleft palate which meant that the English words she knew she could not say properly.

Matthew never laughed at Nimraj or teased her, like some of the other children, but he didn't like her at all. She was in his family unit and she got on his nerves. She was a drag. She was about two years younger than him, but she acted like a baby. She never seemed to understand anything, and she struck him as thick. He had to work with her sometimes, and even play with her, because of the way the family unit worked. He avoided her as much as possible, as if she had the plague. He wasn't the only one, either. Most of the time, unless Miss Kendal forced someone to be with her, Nimraj was quite alone.

When Matthew got her into trouble, though, it was quite by accident. At least, he didn't intend anything nasty to happen to her – it wasn't done deliberately. It was one of those awful things that come about. It came about because Matthew was a good guy, and he couldn't bear to spoil it.

On the afternoon it started, the family unit had been split up into groups for something that was known as "creative play". Each group of children was given something to do or make that was good fun, but meant to teach you something too. Matthew's group was given a kit of technical Lego and told to make a toy that worked. Matthew, naturally, was in charge and all the ideas, as usual, came from him.

It wasn't his choice, but Nimraj was in the group. There were five of them – three boys and two girls. They were meant to operate as a team. As nobody else had a clue about what to make, Matthew decided on a traction engine. The two other boys did the simple bit – the body – while Matthew worked out the gearing, and where to position the motor and the driving belts. Sally, the other girl, helped a little, although she didn't seem that interested. Nimraj just looked on.

Matthew enjoyed himself. It felt good being the boss, and he knew they'd have a fabulous toy to show the rest of the unit by the end of the session. They did and everyone admired it. Matthew and his team wound up the motor, set the traction engine down on the shiny wooden floor, and let it go. It trundled along beautifully, bright red and yellow. It even climbed over small obstacles placed in its path. At hometime, the group had not quite dismantled it entirely when the bell went, and Miss Kendal asked Matthew if he could stay and put the kit away properly. He smiled at the wheels, cogs and motor scattered on the floor among the group, and said he could. He lived quite close to school and nobody would mind if he was a few minutes late.

It was when the other children had gone and his teacher had left the room that the accident happened. One of the gear-wheels dropped from his hand as he was reaching for the moulded hole where it fitted in the box. It rolled away. As he watched, amused at first, it changed direction. It began to run towards the equipment cupboard – a huge, tall, heavy one with a small gap at the bottom. Matthew had hardly time to squeak – and no time at all to act – before it disappeared.

Matthew felt hollow, vaguely sick. The cog was an important one if you were making up a gear chain. He knew that there would be trouble. The technical Lego set was the best thing in the school and not many kids were allowed to touch it. It was posh and very expensive. He almost panicked.

By the time Miss Kendal came back, though, he had pulled himself together. He had stopped peering frantically underneath the cupboard and had gone back to the box. He had packed the rest of the kit away and put the tray with the missing gear wheel at the bottom. Unless someone wanted to build something fairly difficult, they might not notice it for ages.

For the next few days in school, Matthew was uncomfortable. He was filled with fear every time a special period was announced. He tried out various excuses in his head for the missing wheel. Although each family unit had a "creative play" session every so often, the technical Lego was not used, not even by Matthew's set. At first it seemed uncanny, then he relaxed. It was, after all, not a kit they brought out a lot in case it got spoiled, or broken. In the end the tension went away. He forgot all about it and the holidays came.

Like all bad shocks, the shock over the Lego came out of the blue. It was four days after the new term had started, and nothing could have been further from Matthew's mind. It happened when the playtime bell had rung.

As the kids started moving noisily out of the room, Miss Kendal called Matthew over to her table.

"Matthew," she said, pleasantly. "Could you spare me a minute, please? I've got a problem you might be able to help me with."

Matthew smiled with pleasure. He liked the way the teachers talked to him. They treated him like a grown-up.

"Yes Miss," he said. "Of course I can. What's the problem?"

Miss Kendal smiled then because she knew he was trying to sound like a grown-up, too. They understood each other.

"It's the technical Lego kit," she said. "There's a very important piece missing and I wondered if you might just remember as far back as last term, before the holidays."

Matthew did ... suddenly, in a powerful rush. He had forgotten the whole incident but it came roaring back. He opened his mouth, gasping.

Miss Kendal, though, hadn't finished. She went on, pleasantly. "You see, as far as I know, Matthew," she said, "a group that you were in played with it last. And I suspect that one of them lost the piece, or took it even, and didn't mention it. What do you think?"

Matthew was blushing like a beetroot. It was a dead giveaway. Miss Kendal frowned.

"You're very red, dear," she said. "I'm not blaming you, you know. I know you'd never do a thing like that. I thought perhaps that one of the less sensible ones ..."

"But I was in charge of packing it," Matthew gasped. It was brilliant, as an excuse. It covered up his blushing completely. He hadn't meant to make an excuse, it had just come to his lips. Miss Kendal smiled affectionately.

"Oh you're such a good boy, Matthew," she said.

"You never try to excuse yourself, or cover up mistakes. You're such a good boy."

Matthew nodded. What could he say? Miss Kendal went on, seriously.

"Now I'm not blaming anyone, dear, but it is quite important. Do you remember anything about it? Did one of the children take the part? Or lose it? It is very pretty to look at. Nimraj was one of the group, wasn't she? Could it have been her, do you think?"

To Matthew, it seemed daft. Why Nimraj? She didn't give a hoot about the Lego. She hadn't been interested even in making the traction engine. She'd just sat there like a lump – as usual. But why argue? If Miss Kendal wanted to think like that there was nothing he could do about it. It certainly got him off the hook.

"Well I suppose so, Miss," he said. "I mean, she was one of the group. I suppose she could have wanted it for an ornament, or something. She is a bit strange."

"Ah I'm glad you agree." said Miss Kendal. "It certainly seems the most likely answer to me. Poor little thing, she is terribly deprived. Could you stay for a while after school today, dear? Just for a few minutes?"

"Sure," said Matthew. "I mean, yes, Miss Kendal. Why?"

She shook her head and looked at her watch.

"Help! You'd better get out to play," she said. "You've only got a few minutes left. And thanks for all your help, Matthew. You are a good boy."

On and off throughout the rest of the day, Matthew caught himself thinking about what had happened. He felt a little uncomfortable because he'd burnt his boats. He would never be able to dream up a story now, come up with an explanation one day as to where the gear-wheel really was – lost but not for ever! He also felt a little uncomfortable about getting off so lightly – but he hadn't told any lies or anything. Miss Kendal had been so certain he'd had nothing to do with it that, after a while, he somehow felt she must be right. After all, he was trusted. He was a good guy. He caught himself smiling with relief. How fantastically easy it had been! He'd got away with it – just like that.

At the end of the day, though, Matthew got another shock. He went along to the headteacher's room, as Miss Kendal had told him earlier, and found his teacher already there ... with Nimraj.

Matthew stood in the large, light room feeling very confused and awkward. He had not expected this at all. It had not occurred to him that this was why they had wanted him to stay. His mouth was dry and his palms were wet. He was nervous.

Mrs Mansell – a small, grey-haired woman – was

not a frightening headteacher. She had sat Nimraj in a nice armchair, despite the fact that she looked so grubby, and given her a biscuit and a glass of milk. She offered Matthew one, but he refused, stammering slightly. She pointed to a chair and he sat down. He stole a glance at Nimraj, but she was looking at the floor.

"Well, Matthew," said Mrs Mansell. "Miss Kendal has told me all about everything, and I've spoken to Nimraj here. But she is rather shy, as you know. Could you tell us all again just what happened that afternoon?"

Matthew glanced at Mrs Mansell, then at Miss Kendal. His face was a painful red. This wasn't fair, it was terrible. What did they expect him to say? After a fairly long silence, Miss Kendal prompted him.

"Matthew told me that Nimraj was a member of the group which last played with the technical Lego kit," she said. "He said he thought Nimraj may have taken it."

There was a noise from Nimraj. It was not a word, just a noise. Matthew could not look at her. Then there was another pause.

Mrs Mansell said, "Nimraj appears to disagree, Matthew. Are you sure she took it?"

"No!" said Matthew. "No, I didn't say that! It just seems ... I mean, Miss Kendal ... I just said she was in the group, that's all."

"And that she may have thought it was a nice ornament," said Miss Kendal. "That's right, isn't it. dear? That's what you thought?"

Matthew did not reply. He moved his eyes sideways under his eyelids, until he could see Nimraj without her knowing. She was staring at him, her eyes big and brown in her pale, calm face. He felt ashamed. But he felt angry too, angry at her. She was so useless. She was so quiet and so calm. He hated her.

After a minute or so, Mrs Mansell made a noise in her throat. She stood up behind her big table.

"Well, Nimraj," she said. "I think you'd better run along now, dear. We'll see you in the morning. You run along now, dear, there's a good girl."

Nimraj stared at her, but she did not speak. She got up from her armchair and left the room. She did not look back.

After she had gone Miss Kendal gave a small, nervous laugh.

"What a sad little thing Nimraj is," she said.

Matthew blurted out, "What's going to happen? What are you gong to do to her?"

The Headmistress and the teacher exchanged glances.

"Oh nothing, dear," said Mrs Mansell. "What could we do, do you think? We're just trying to arrive at the truth, that's all. Nothing terrible's going to happen. No harm will come of it."

Miss Kendal said, "But you do think she may have taken it, don't you, Matthew? You can speak honestly now, dear, now that she's gone. You do think she might have taken it? For an ornament, or something like that?"

Their eyes were boring into him. He nodded miserably. It wasn't fair.

"I suppose so," he said. "I suppose she could have done."

Nimraj was not at school next day. Matthew noticed immediately, when they went to their family unit room after prayers. He'd been dreading meeting her, and she wasn't there. He was very relieved. It made life a whole lot easier.

At lunchtime, when he was setting off for home, Miss Kendal had a word with him.

"It look as though that proves it, Matt," she said. "I feel terribly sorry for the poor little thing, but it looks as if she's admitted it by staying away. I expect she'll be back soon. She'll soon get over it."

Matthew was cautious.

"But you said nothing was going to happen to her anyway." he said. "No one would hurt her if she came to school. They wouldn't tell her off, would they? It's stupid to stay away."

Miss Kendal laughed. "That's right," she said. "Stupid. She's probably a bit ashamed though. She'll soon be back."

"I suppose so," said Matthew. "She is silly, though." He put on his most grown-up voice. "Poor little thing," he said. "She's so deprived." He went home to lunch feeling somehow quite pleased with himself.

By the time he went back to school, Matthew had forgotten all about the thing. He'd had a good lunch, and by halfway through it any lingering worry he might have had had passed. Everyone, but everyone, had come out of it all right. He was whistling happily, without a care in the world, when he spotted Nimraj behind a wall.

On a whim, he shouted to her.

"Hey!" he called. "Hey, Nimraj! Where were you this morning? Come here!"

They weren't far from the school gates, less than two hundred metres. It was a tumbledown area, of boarded up shops and houses. Nimraj was standing on a patch of weedy ground. She did not move, or reply.

"Hey!" he called again. "Come here. I want to talk to you."

Nimraj looked him full in the face, then turned away. She started to move off, almost running.

Matthew was annoyed. 'Stupid girl,' he thought, 'I want to help you. I've got good news.' He started trotting after her.

When Nimraj saw him coming, she speeded up her run. She looked over her shoulder then put her head down. Matthew was exhilarated. He liked a good chase. She had a start, but he was very fast. In less than two minutes he had her cornered between two jagged walls. She was panting, but he was hardly blown.

"What's up, you daft thing?" he said. "Why were you running away? Why weren't you at school this morning?"

Nimraj stared at him, panting. Her big brown eyes were almost black. She seemed afraid of him. It shook Matthew a bit. She really seemed afraid.

He reached a hand out.

"I won't hurt you, Nimraj," he said gently. "What are you afraid of?"

She shrank away from his touch until she was almost crouching. Matthew drew his hand back.

"I won't hurt you." he repeated. "I'm a g ..." He almost said 'a good guy'. Then he almost blushed. "You must come back to school," he said. "Everybody's worrying. No one's going to hurt you, Nimraj. The Lego thing's forgotten. Nobody's going to hurt you."

She started to cry. Tears began to pour out of her eyes in torrents. A look of amazing pain was on her face, something that Matthew had never seen in his life before. Her face seemed to somehow crumble, every muscle was twisted, tortured. She opened her mouth and a low, awful, tearing noise came out of it. Matthew was horrified. His eyes widened. He had a sudden, overwhelming sense of guilt. It was his fault. He knew it, clearly and completely. It was all his fault.

Nimraj said, "You have hurt me. You. You will hurt me. You. You have hurt me."

She leaned against the wall and covered her face with one arm. The awful, tearing noise went on.

Matthew stood beside her in an equal agony. He looked at her bent, shuddering head and saw her clearly for the very first time. Nimraj. Pathetic, helpless and alone. Confused, unhappy and lost. He was not a good guy after all. He was not a hero. He was filled with shame and horror. 'Good guys,' he thought, 'don't hurt the weak.'

He knew what he was going to do, but he didn't know what to do first. He ought to stay with Nimraj, to try to help and comfort her. But he didn't know how. Without a word, he crept away without her knowing it. He walked into school, pale and trembling, and went into the family unit. Miss Kendal was there, alone because the bell had not yet gone. He walked straight to her table.

"Gosh, Matthew," she said. "What's all this? Matthew?" Her voice had changed. "You don't look well."

"The Lego, Miss," he said. "I've just remembered. It's under that cupboard there. It rolled under after the lesson."

"Good Lord," she said. "How amazing. But your voice, Matthew, there's something wrong with your voice."

"The cupboard, Miss. It's underneath the cupboard." His voice was strangled, shaking.

"Where Nimraj dropped it, then?" asked Miss Kendal. "Is that it, dear?"

He looked at her, with difficulty and his eyes filled with tears.

"Where I did, Miss," he said. "Poor Nimraj wasn't even there. You made me ... No. I told a lie. I dropped it there. I was afraid."

He saw Miss Kendal through his blurry eyes. She looked at her table top. After a short while she said, "Oh Matthew. What a good boy you are. You really are such a very good boy."

Her voice was very odd, but Matthew was not there to hear it. He'd gone to look for Nimraj on the wasteground. He had gone to see if he could find her.